Love Takes a Bow

Other Books by Dan Gilmore

SHORT STORIES AND POETRY

Season Tickets

NOVEL

A Howl for Mayflower

Love Takes a Bow

new & collected poems

Dan Gilmore

IMAGO
PRESS
TUCSON ARIZONA

Published in the United States of America by:

Imago Press
3710 East Edison
Tucson AZ 85716
www.imagobooks.com

Library of Congress Control Number: 2010926756

Book and Cover Design by Leila Joiner
Cover photograph: stage © Martin Fischer

ISBN 978-1-935437-18-5
ISBN 1-935437-18-6

Printed in the United States of America on Acid-Free Paper

Acknowledgments

Special thanks to Leila Joiner, Tom Speer, and Patricia Harmon.

for JoAn

Contents

PART SIX

With poetry we come to love

—Tess Gallagher

Dear Reader

I offer you my poems
and feel like Baryshnikov
leaping across the stage.
I bound high as I can
for your nods, bow humbly
for your smiles and breathy umms.
Yet I know that any approval
you may bestow will leave me
wondering if you have lowered
your standards. I know
these words are only flickers
of awakening in this darkness
that is my life. But I'll continue
to write them because,
like the woodpecker pecking
at a tree doggedly searching
for tidbits of sustenance,
this is what I do.

PART ONE

Love Takes a Bow

At the end of the play, the curtain closes
and Love takes a bow—exhausted Love,
glorious Love, suspicious Love—while
behind the curtain, Anger and Fear wait
their turn to receive their ovation.

There is a moment when Love is tempted
to leap headlong into the audience and drown
in adulation. But possessed by self-restraint,
Love smiles sweetly and shushes the audience.

When silence is complete, Love parts the curtain
and with a come-hither finger summons Anger and Fear.
Anger stands at Love's right, frowning, trying
not to smile. Fear cringes on Love's left.
Love holds their hands and the three bow together.

Suddenly the audience is possessed by
inexplicable passion. They rip off their clothes,
fondle and kiss. Love, Anger, and Fear bow
again and again. Something wonderful is happening here.

Panning for Gold

Can't sleep. I sit at the kitchen counter
before a tall white vase holding spring's
first iris and next to it, a blue bowl piled
high with the last of this season's
oranges. I stare into the flower and

remember long ago on Route 66
a roadside stand with a sign, *Pan For Gold
25 Cents.* A whiskered man in muddy boots
dipped the pan in the sluice and showed me
how hope looked. When I found

a small nugget and gave it to my mother,
I thought I'd saved us from every bad thing.
I wanted to stay forever panning for gold, but
she said we couldn't afford another nugget.

Now I peel an orange, old and wrinkled
but at its peak of sweetness. I sniff
the peel, taste a wedge, hold its sweetness
on my tongue and think of the time I made a list
of a hundred things I wanted to accomplish

before I died. Real nuggets, it seems,
cost not a quarter but a life, a life that produced
the miracle of me sitting here with a newborn iris
and this bowl overflowing with old sweet oranges.

No Self

I've given up. The pilgrimage is over.
I've wasted too many years looking
for my one true Self. I've come to accept
that in the opera called my life there's
no top billing, only a cast of thousands,
all shameless amateurs bent on playing
me and scoffing at the idea of team play.

Some lie and cheat, some writhe in pain.
Some can't stop laughing. Some are men,
some women. Some would shoot their mother,
others would die to save her. Some hide
in terror. Others swagger like generals
inflated with grandiosity. Some are prophets,
some loose cannons. And I never know
who's going to show up next.

So, if you think of me, think of this gaggle
of bumbling actors who jostle and goose
their way forward to claim a moment
of your attention, a smile, a pat—
an undisciplined gathering with no scripts
and no plot, nothing except a puzzling
persistence seeking immortality
on the crumbling stage of my imagination.

World's Shortest Play

(for Cynthia and Joe)

I was Hansel, Susan was Gretel, Big Jackie
the mother, Snarly Carla, the witch. Shy Sarah
opened the curtain. The rest were village people
or witch's helpers. My mother refused to come.
She believed being someone else was a sin.
But when Sarah opened the curtain, there she was,
first row, stern, holding her Bible. I lost focus.
Ten seconds into the play, I saw Big Jackie
in the wings, that comforting smile of hers
and delivered my line that came at the end
of the play: "Oh, look, here's Mother."
Jackie and the village people stampeded
on stage to hug Susan and me for killing
Snarly Carla who had yet to appear. Sarah, confused
as usual, lowered the curtain. Susan stood
gape-mouthed in her starched Gretel dress,
and Snarly Carla said "Shit" so loud it silenced
everyone except the audience who applauded
while Big Jackie morphed into a plump,
moist, hugging angel. She hugged the village people
and Snarly Carla and all of Carla's evil helpers.
She found Sarah and me hiding behind the curtain
and hugged us too. She helped Miss Kemper stop crying.
And from all this came my first glimmer that
what was happening was the real play. It would
go on forever—helpers and followers, shy curtain pullers,
tearful leaders, scowling mothers, foolish bumblers,
mean witches, angels and onlookers—all of us bound
together by hope, ideals, folly, terror and unexpected love.

Happiest Black White Man Alive

It's 1954. San Bernardino, California. The smoke's still clearing from a race riot down on Mt. Vernon Avenue. Bad scene—couple of black kids killed by two white cops and the place split open—police dogs, clubs, fire hoses, shops burned, cars tipped over—and I'm a nineteen year-old white drummer, and this black dude named Ray Byrd—best tenor sax player in town, fronts his own big band—calls me on a Thursday afternoon. His words run together like one long chesty growl. Says he's a friend of Scott somebody who played tenor with Johnny Jones big band when I played drums with Jones, that he, Byrd, is gigging at a place called Little Harlem on the west side just behind the Santa Fe station and just east of Mt. Vernon, and he's been playing there on weekends for a year but last week he lost his drummer for busting a cop's nose, and anyway Scott what-is-that-dude's-name says I can hold a groove, play decent fills and read charts, and he's found a sub for Saturday but Friday is still a problem. You open?

And I'm thinking, this is gold. Me getting a gig with the best band in town. Then I'm thinking I'm scared shitless, don't know if I can cut it with Byrd's musicians. I'm not in the same league. Then I'm thinking I don't know about me being white and playing in an all-black band in an all-black club. I'm thinking black folks are angry, that to them I'd sound like Lawrence fucking Welk.

"Wait," I say. "Ain't your band all black? Ain't this Little Harlem an all-black club?"

"You got a problem with that?"

"No, no, no. I'm cool with it, but man, I'm white. I don't think I could pass."

"Pass what?"

"I mean, dude, look at it—I mean imagine me, the only white guy in the place, playing drums—not just, I don't know, trombone—but drums, man."

"Okay, I got you imagined. Little white dude sittin' up there playing drums."

"I mean won't that piss black folks off? You know what I'm saying—that thing about black folks got rhythm. You dig?"

"I seen some black folks don't know blues from a polka."

I look down at my skin. It seems to be growing whiter by the minute. When I talk I sound like Sergeant Preston. "Yeah," I say, "but doesn't that get switched around in black folk's minds to something like, *only* black folks got rhythm?"

Byrd makes a noise that sounds like he finds this funny. "You a little scared of being white, eh?"

"I'm talking about black rage, man. Hell, I'd feel it if I worked my ass off all week, got duded up to go out and the drummer turned out to be me."

"Maybe you can put on some of that black shoe polish."

"I'm serious, man. But, hey, don't—I want to do the gig, for sure. I mean I dig your band, I mean it would be an honor, you know, how it swings and, you know—and if me being white is—"

"If you're as good as my man Scott says you is, then you got nothing to worry 'bout. You that good?"

"Good? Yeah, maybe—I guess, but your band's not just—you know, good—it's great. "

"Gig begins at nine, ends at two. Be there by eight-thirty. You get fifty plus tips."

"You okay with me being—then, hey, I'm cool—"

"Brothers and sisters get a few drinks in them, hear our sound, they more worried about gettin' down and gettin' some lovin' than what color the drummer is. You give 'em that money beat, that back beat on two and four, they ain't gonna hassle you. Besides, it's dark in there. We'll keep the lights low for you."

So I spend the rest of the night listening to cats like Art Blakey, Max Roach, and Elvin Jones. I'm listening with my sticks in my hand, trying to understand that special thing they got. I mean it ain't just technique or independence or musicality. I have that. It's something I don't have a name for, but my balls know. When they hear it, they begin to quiver. Maybe its name is just "black," and my white balls know I don't have it.

Next night I head south on Mt. Vernon to Fifth Avenue, take a left and drive three blocks to a flat brick building about half the size of a football field. The parking lot is twice the size of the building and already almost full. Unloading, I hear laughter, some cat calls and Count Basie's band playing on the juke box.

As soon as I walk in with my bass drum, all the noise stops. Basie does one of his endings, and the place is a tomb. I look around for the bandstand and spot it in the far corner. Byrd is there. He waves me over. And while I walk I'm aware I am walking like a white man, sorta stiff-legged with a starched back. I trip over my own feet and do a little hop, trying to make it look like I did it on purpose. I try showing that black, swaying thing but feel like a performing seal.

I hear whispers. *Who dat white kid? White kid can't get down. Heard Tucker's in jail. Got a real drummer for tomorrow night.* Someone tries to crack a joke. The punch line is, *Preacher, I don't know who called your drummer a motherfucker, what I want to know is who called that motherfucker a drummer*—and everybody laughs.

"They just having some fun," Byrd says. He tells me to drive around the building and park next to the side door to finish unloading.

Every time I walk out, I smell raw sewage, smoke from the Santa Fe station, hear locomotives gaining speed, hear sirens, see police patrol cars. And I know I am in the heart of the ghetto where folks work shit jobs if they work at all and spend a week's wages to escape to a place outside their real world, to a place called Little Harlem. And I know also I'm in a place I don't want to be.

But when I walk inside it feels different, nowhere near the ghetto or the Santa Fe station, nowhere near San Bernardino or anywhere I've ever been. There's red, blue, and purple lights, the sweet scents of perfumes and liquors, people already standing on the dance floor, waiting. White folks wait until they get good and drunk before they get out on the dance floor. Then they move like they had a broomstick up their butts. But here, twenty minutes before we start, there's a buzz. Women dressed in their finest silk dresses and high heels, men with polished Florsheims and silk suits, all moving their bodies as if something caged inside is trying to get loose. My hands are clammy.

The first set goes okay, mainly medium tempo stuff. A trio called Alice, Faye, and Robin sing every *my-man-done-left-me* song, every *all-I-want-is-my-baby-back-so-my-heart-can-sing* song. And I'm laying down the money beat on two and four. And it feels good at the end when folks whoop and jive and clap and do that Amen church response thing when Byrd asks if they're enjoying themselves. And I'm grateful that he never looks at me or says who I am or what I am.

From the bandstand I watch the cigarette smoke, trapped by a ten-foot high unvented ceiling, snake its way through the crowd, and I think *This ain't half bad.* I'm playing in Little Harlem with Byrd's big band, and I'm laying down a sharp backbeat to slow blues, doing the triplet thing on the high hat, the left hand snapping off the snare on two and four. What was I thinking? This is easy money. Me being white don't mean shit to these people. Nobody except me seems to notice.

At the break I don't leave the bandstand. Byrd pulls up a chair next to me and says, "We generally turn it up on the second set."

"What's that mean?" I say. "Faster, louder, longer, what?"

"Yeah," Byrd says.

I look around, try to be cool, nod to a couple of women as they strut by in their slit skirts, net stockings, and high heels.

Byrd says, "We play C-Jam Blues at about one-eighty beats per minute for the whole set."

"Great tune," I say, but I'm thinking I've never played that fast for that long in my life. I'm thinking you play that fast for that long, and your body begins to freeze up. It starts with your thighs filling with sand, then you can't move your feet, can't even feel your feet, then a steel belt wraps around your back and chest and you can't breathe. After that your whole body turns to stone and your arms and hands refuse to move. And you're sitting there like a rusted-out statue of a guy who has just received a two-hundred-volt electric charge.

"You think you can handle that?" Byrd says.

And I say, "That's cool, man."

So we start the second set. Byrd counts off C-Jam—one, two, one, two, ugh, ugh. And we're off. The whole band is playing the lead, then the head bone guy solos for five minutes, then the piano, then a trumpet, then Byrd starts his job. I'm keeping up but I'm working my ass off. This is like a hundred-yard-dash guy running five miles. I think I'm pushing the beat, digging deeper into the groove, but the bass player turns and gives me the eye, the eye every drummer can read and would slit his throat not to see, the eye that says, *You're dragging, man.* And suddenly I realize I'm playing on one and three instead of two and four. This is the worst thing a drummer can do. This can get you shot. Worse yet, it's about the whitest thing in the whole world, the shit you hear in country music. So I get back on two and four and try harder, but trying harder gets me nothing but stiffer. And I'm counting to myself—not feeling, just counting from one to four over and over again. Twenty-five minutes pass. I have to make it for another twenty. Byrd is honking away and I'm trying to find something to take my mind off my body, something to free me up as much as those dancers on the floor. They are moving in ways I've never seen anyone move before, sexy ways I never knew bodies could move—sliding here, twisting there, shaking, thrusting, and jiggling all at the same time. And it looks so easy, so effortless. I want their freedom, their abandon. I want all of what they got.

Byrd is on his knees, his horn moving up and down like a gold cock humping the air. His ascending gleeful sounds make my hairs stand on end. Now he's on his back, playing a line that sounds like the growl when he talks. Blue and purple and red cigarette smoke snakes its way through the room through a thousand perfumes, thick bourbons, Scotches, all mixed with barrels of face sweat, breast sweat, crotch sweat, fishnet thigh sweat, and the dancing doesn't stop, and it won't stop as long as I kept hitting the back beat and keep that bass man from looking at me like I just tore his soul from his body. I'm scared I'm gonna reverse the beat again and the whole scene will stop in disgust because the white drummer kid just blew the fuse on a thousand black souls because he hit on one and three instead of two and four.

I'm counting and praying I can breathe-in that black thing, suck in some of that electric buzz snaking around me. At this moment I'll give my life just to take a twenty-minute vacation from jerking off atop this ticking metronome of white logic.

Now some folks have stopped dancing and gathered close to listen and watch because Byrd has left his body and is playing higher and louder and so beautiful, man, he is building a raging fire in the collective soul of Little Harlem. Then suddenly one of Byrd's big yellow eyes pops open and looks at me. It's that *Show-'em what-you-got* eye, that *Time-to-take-your-first-solo* eye. And all I can think about is how my body is hardening up and how pale I've been all my life.

Byrd gives a sign, and the band is silent. People stop dancing and move in closer to see what the white boy's got. The only sound in the entire universe is my high hat going on two and four and snappy little white bread, high school marching band sounds of my brushes on the snare. I am praying for an idea, a place to run, for Byrd to see how much I don't want to do this. I look at him and give the signal for the band to come back in, but Byrd just smiles and nods his head. I hate the fucker.

Then I feel my body begin to relax a little. I kick the bass drum [BOOM], switch to sticks and start this double-time riff off the left hand, and in my head I'm hearing those sweet sounds of Blakey, Roach, and Webb. No, not in my head at all but in my body. These three saints have taken possession of my body and I'm playing around the set with more ease than I've ever known. And what I'm playing ain't white.

My right hand moves back and forth from the small tom to the big tom. My right foot echoes that sound on the bass, shit I've never done before. Where it comes from I don't know, but it definitely ain't coming from me. I'm being played by all the cats I've listened to all my life, trying to understand that thing they have that I don't have. It's black, all right, and my balls are dancing. My right hand leaps to the ride cymbal, back to the snare. Good shit is happening all over and my bass is keeping the [BOOM/BOOM ba-ba BOOM] thing going like a heartbeat. I look up and heads are moving. Some cats in the band are snapping their fingers and moving their shoulders to my beat.

I move deeper into myself, let something there that's screaming take over. And we're all back in some jungle-part of ourselves, the center of the fire, cinders flaring, life flowing from a place where there's too much happiness, where nothing is good or bad, just IS and this sound I'm making is ALL there is, and I give the eye back to Byrd, who is wrinkled-eyed smiling, and I hit this final lick, pause and [BOOM] kick the band back in. The trumpets squeal that high shit. Bones moan like they been kicked in the tes...ti...cles, and saxes join in with a rocking staccato riff that sounds like one of those Santa Fe trains going full-out, and the whole band echoes the same riff higher and higher until it's impossible to go any higher. Im-fucking-possible. Then the lead trumpet goes up a whole octave and holds that high note while the rest of the band lays down the riff, louder and louder. And I think the trumpet player's head is going to explode if he doesn't get off it, but he holds it, beat after beat, measure after measure, holds it while this freaked-out woman is snaking around on the floor, humping the air, holding her breasts, possessed. It's so beautiful, man, my eyes start to well up as the band heads home and everyone is grooving and it doesn't surprise me when I look down and see my hands are black, arms too, all of me has turned black, and pains and fears have slipped out the back door, and there's nothing left except all that's good and pure and me smiling so big it hurts, 'cause I never felt this full before. Something inside me is sliding and shaking and twisting and jiggling all at the same time, and my body knows what Blakey, Roach, and Jones had, and at that moment I am the happiest black white man alive.

ZENO'S PARADOX

My world changed for the better one evening
when a college-bound girl named Linda spread
her legs just enough for my hand to explore
the creamy smoothness of her inner thigh.

Then suddenly she locked her knees, sat erect,
pushed me back and in that sad way women can do,
said she wasn't interested in a man who couldn't read.
I stared silently at my lustful hand, its pudgy,
useless fingers. She must have sensed
my shame. "Not forever, silly," she said,
"just till you learn to read." So I enrolled
in three adult bonehead classes, and by summer's end
had read Russell's *History of Western Philosophy*.

"Prove it," she said when I called. So we sat
in the front seat of my car, my right hand resting
lightly on her knee, my sweaty left hand holding
a copy of Russell's book and I read a passage
about Zeno's Paradox, which pointed out
the impossibility of ever really touching something
even though it's obvious we do. My voice shook,

but I hit every word. And when I finished,
Linda asked where I stood on Zeno's Paradox.
I said, in theory Zeno was right. You can never
pick a peach, but in real life its juicy sweetness
seemed real enough. "That's the paradox," she said,
as she slid down into the seat and her knees parted.
"Don't you know what paradox means, silly?" And
this small opening marked the beginning
of my journey into the world of letters.

PART TWO

GROUP SHOWER

Cold, naked boys huddle together
without touching, shivering, pale fingers
covering shrunken penises as the teacher
displays a jock strap draped on a stick
and warns about the horrors of jock mold.
Water and steam engulf them,
but they are still cold. Their lanky
blue bodies stand like iced statues
on a fog-blanketed night, as if a sweet
naiveté has frozen them, made them
impenetrable. Here in this cold steam
a boy is born into a secret brotherhood.
He senses his death but doesn't know
his life. Forever he will invent and reinvent
himself, polish the surface of himself,
never sure what's his and what's theirs.
He will try to fly and discover wings
are made of ice. He will forever
wander the thorny path that circles
his life, but he will never find
his way to the fire.

SHARING STARS

We stood facing one another—
caved-in chests, baggy pants,
boxing gloves that reached
past our knees. You're ugly,
Joe said. Shut up, I said, Pay
attention and watch my footwork.
Always the teacher, I flicked
three flashing left jabs. Now
try to hit me. I saw his right
coming but before I could move,
my jaw wrapped around his glove,
my knees gave way and I was falling
floating through an orange
and red galaxy of stars,
pleased with my distant face
how perfectly it cushioned my landing.

Then I was looking into Joe's eyes.
You all right? Nice shot, I said, then
told him about the stars. Really? he said.
I thought that only happened in cartoons.
He helped me up, stood before me and said,
Hit me. Why? I asked. I want to see
the stars, he said. At the time
this made perfect sense. So I hit him.
He's out cold, eyes closed,
a silly smile on his lips. Finally
he opened one eye and said,
Amazing, friggin' amazing. That

was when I knew how much I loved him.
But he went one way, I another,
and years later, when I heard he'd drowned
trying to rescue his girlfriend from a rip tide,
I felt I'd betrayed him, that I'd failed

to teach him about water and girls.
Then I remembered his wanting to see
my stars. I filled my bathtub, intending
to stay under water long enough to know
what he must have felt. I imagined clinging
to a limp body, loving her so much that I
couldn't let go, that I would give my life
to save hers. But my lungs ached, and without
willing it, I sat up and sucked in air and bawled out
You bastard. What I really wanted was to have him
stand still, facing me with that stupid smile on his face
and let me hit him as hard as I could.

Double Bubble

cost a nickel that year so
Arlene Sibernickle and I shared
a piece. I paid three
cents, she two. We chewed it
for a whole school year, tucked
away in a tackbox, hers one week,
mine the next. And at the end
of the year, the night before she
moved, I scooted under the back fence
of the Baseline Drive-in
and turned on a speaker. We sat
behind the chainlink fence,
watched Fred Astaire
and Ginger Rogers dance
and shared our gum for the last time.

Walking back to her house,
we took turns chewing the gum.
We tried to decide who should have custody
but couldn't. Then Arlene said we should
bury it near her mailbox. We said
our goodbyes, placed it in its box
and stood looking at its small grave,
feeling sad. Halfway home
I went back to reclaim it,
but Arlene had been there first.
I almost knocked on her door
but realized nothing was going
to change. The gum was gone
forever. So I went back
to the drive-in and watched
Fred and Ginger dance some more.
On that night I decided
I'd dance my life away
with someone like Ginger.

I decided that most relationships
with girls had to be less painful
than the one I had with Arlene.

THE ONE TIME MY FATHER GOT HIS WAY

He held the two-by-four he'd just cut
to the space it was supposed to fill.
He'd cut it two feet short. "Came up
a little short," he said. My mother sneered.
That sneer usually meant he'd slump
into the house and turn on the TV,
but this time he tried again.

The next board was longer than the first
but still short by a foot. "Shit," he said,
and my mother rolled her eyes, a sign
of complete disdain. But even then
he didn't give in. It took weeks,
but he built a new, smaller porch to fit
his two short boards. And one summer

evening, the three of us sat
in our downsized porch—my mother
with arms folded, fingers making
zeros on her elbows, me squeezed
in the middle, shoulders pinched
so far forward I felt like a closed book,
my father wedged in sideways
smiling or maybe grimacing. I never
knew what he was thinking. But that night
I hoped he wasn't thinking
about remodeling the whole house.

Buzz

He was the "me-first," bouncing, fearless type.
Yelped and leapt at his leash, urged me
to crawl under Mr. Anderson's chain link fence
to run across old man Jeffrey's forbidden field.
He slept by my side on his back, legs
straight up, trembling as if holding back
a boulder about to crush us. I never felt safer.
Since those years, I've crawled under

my share of forbidden fences, escaped
an avalanche of falling stones, and I still
remember the caring way my father lowered
him back-first into his grave and rolled
a heavy stone over him. I think of him there,
holding up that stone, protecting me in ways
an angel might. And it seems important
to honor him—a lighted candle, a small

parade, this poem read aloud to friends.
Odd to think I'm the only one alive
who watched him sleep, the only one
who felt completely safe in his presence.
Odd to wonder if I've come close
to giving anyone the same gift.

SCAVENGING WITH MY FATHER

Remember when
we found things
in that dump, pieces
of toast, a pocket
filled with stones?

Remember that broken
mirror with gold trim
next to that three-legged
old dog with pups?

Remember her watery
eyes, her skin graveled
by ticks, those pups
sucking her empty
crushed-grape teats?

Don't you remember
how you gave
her water
and we watched
her lick life
back into those pups?

I remember.
You must.
Please remember.

That's when you
mumbled something
about how much
that old dog
loved those pups,
how the best love
comes from broken
and wrecked bodies.

Heartbreak Hotel

I stuck a tattered Elvis wig on my father's head,
shoved my old guitar into his hands, turned up
the volume and, camera in hand, urged him
to mouth the words and shake his hips to Elvis's
Heartbreak Hotel. But he just stood still like a
stuffed mastodon. I shoved him to make him move
even just a little. I don't know what I wanted.
Maybe the two of us could go camping or something
stupid like that. Then, just before the record ended,

his eyes welled with tears as if he'd glimpsed
someone he used to love in a crowd. I snapped
a picture of that expression and in the flash
his eyes clouded over and his smile vanished.
He took off the wig and sat for a long time
looking at his feet, rubbing that fake hair between
his fingers. Thirty years later I still don't know

what he was thinking. I'm looking at that picture now,
that expression, and I'm remembering the monkey
in the Psych 101 movie, how he suddenly saw
the connection between his stick and the unreachable
banana, and I'm wondering if it's possible that,
in those few seconds, my father glimpsed the possibilities
of himself, realized he could be someone different.
Before he could grab hold of it, it slipped away
and he felt even more alone. I think of us now,

father and son who shared nothing, alone under the stars,
our tiny campfire lighting a small piece of darkness.

My Father's Toolbox

I was past being impressed by anything
an adult could do when he talked
me into going to the dump. I kicked
at a stiff work glove, threw a couple
of stones at some gulls and said
I'd wait in the car. He held up
a rusted pair of pliers and a drill bit
and said he couldn't believe anyone
would throw something like this
away. I said I couldn't believe
he could say something that dumb.

At home, he put the pliers and bit
in a box he'd made of scrap wood—squeaky
hinges, edges worn smooth over the years
by hands rough as files. Nothing useful inside—
a screwdriver with half a handle,
a hammer stained with tar, baby food
jars filled with bent nails, rusted screws,
tangled string. I asked what he planned
to do with all that junk. He shrugged, closed
the box, gave it a pat, and said I'd missed
the point. When he died a few years later,

I threw the toolbox away. I'm alone now,
same age he was when he died,
and I'm sitting in my back yard
like an old dog who stays put
long after his fence has fallen.
There's a rusted gate that's lost
its swing, a ladder no longer safe
for climbing, a patch of weeds
grown large as women's
thighs, and I'm thinking of my father,

wondering when it was he came to understand
how we cling for all we're worth
to that sweet wreckage we call our lives.

First TV

My mother took a moral stand against it,
said television was the work of the devil,
said my father's wanting it showed how
weak he really was. But, for once, he stood
firm. It was a blond GE with a twelve-inch
screen—a blond whore my mother couldn't
have hated more. After supper, we sat on the sofa

in the dark, my mother wedged in the middle,
hands over her ears, back straight, her worn
leather Bible on her lap. My father switched it on.
Roller Derby came at us like a train on fire,
women on skates trying to kill one another—
knees to the midsection, elbows to the neck,
hair pulling, eye gouging. Suddenly my mother

leaned forward and yelled, "Kill her. Oh, kill her.
Hit her in the mouth." She jabbed us with her elbows,
moved to the edge of the sofa. Her Bible lay splayed
at her feet like an injured player. During a commercial
she read aloud from John 12:46. *I am come a light
into the world, that whosoever believeth on me
should not abide in darkness.* "Amen," she said, as the men

took the track. She marked her place with a finger,
sat forward again and yelled, "Kill him, kick him.
That's it. Oh, hurt him." My father excused himself
to get a glass of water. I sat on the floor to escape
her sharp elbow. And, years later, this is the way
I remember her: alone, agitated, the empty space

around her expanding, the wild, festering pleasure
she took in wrestling, boxing, and roller derby, that Bible
always within reach, proof to all that a better place awaited her.

The Lord's Prayer

Our Father who art in heaven...

It has become a kind of game.
My mother tells him I've done
something bad. He unbuckles
his belt and wraps it around
his hand a couple of times.
I lower my trousers and he whips
me until the blood comes.
My mother watches without flinching,
arms folded under her heavy breasts.

Give us this day our daily bread...

When he's gone, I sit on the edge
of the bed. She unbuttons her blouse,
unhooks her bra and holds my head
to her breasts. She pulls me tighter.
She rocks and strokes my head.
She promises she'll never let him
hurt me again. But that's just part
of the game. We know she needs
my blood to justify her hate
for him, to make me into what
she once believed he could be.
She presses me closer, rocks and prays
that I'll never end up like him.

Lead us not into temptation

On Sunday, I'll sit next to her at church,
breathing in scents of lye soap,
face powder, Dentyne, while Jesus,
all bloody, looks down from his cross
at his mother crying at his feet,

making promises she can't keep.
The preacher always says something
about salvation but I know it will
never come. Then we eat the flesh,
drink the blood, and recite the prayer
I know by heart but don't believe—

BLESS MY MOTHER

When a motorist cut me off
and flipped me the finger,
I felt anger flash, I thought
of my mother. In my family
we weren't masters of subtlety
when it came to hating. Her two
favorite sayings were, *Don't get mad,
get even,* and *If a sumbitch
is hiding in his barn, burn it down.*

Mother, I called, and next thing
I knew, she was there, next to me.
She gave my leg a quick pat, leaned
forward into the windshield and said,
Follow that sumbitch. I saw the two
of us dousing his house with gasoline
and him living just long enough
to experience my mother's dreaded finger
of blame wagging in his face as she said,
You die when you mess with my boy.
But the pickup was out of sight, and as quickly

as she appeared, she was gone again. Nice
of her not to hang around, I thought. I hadn't
called on her in a long time. Later, I sat
in my back yard looking up at a sliver
of moon and, as these things often go,
after a while the moon was looking back at me,
and I realized it was a sad smile because
it saw the frightened core of me, the part
no one can protect, the part that still
yearns for something I'll never have.

PART THREE

Wedding Night

I rented a house the morning of our wedding,
a place furnished only with a urine-stained
Goodwill mattress, two dirty quilts, a red plastic cup,
a jar of Nescafe, a small teapot and a spoon.

After picking you up at the Greyhound station,
we stood before the JP in his overheated
office, you ritualistically fingering
your mother's band. I had no ring,
refused to wear one. We vowed our love,
but I had a head cold and refused to kiss you.

Afterwards, we ate burgers at Denny's.
You said your suitcase was filled
with dirty clothes. I said I needed
to grade papers and dropped you off
at the house, promising to pick up
some real coffee, promising things would
get better once I got over my cold.

I drove a block, parked and sat there
for three hours, engine running, windshield
iced over. I flicked my Zippo lighter,
chain smoked, and belched onions. When
I returned at two, found you huddled
against the kitchen radiator, wrapped
in a quilt, red cup filled with coffee
between mittened hands. You asked

if I knew where a laundromat was.
It seemed like a miracle that I did,
a miracle driving you there, ice cracking
under the weight of the car, a miracle
that we sat silently through the wash cycles,
watching your laundry tumble, me trying
to breathe while thinking about the lies
I'd told, the promises I'd never keep.

Morning Civility

Dressed in my surrogate body
I make my way to the kitchen,
a black cat attached to my face.
Oblivious, you take a sip of tea and say,
"Morning. Sleep well?" I want
to confess I'm an impostor,
that the real me hates the sight
of tea, prefers his own damp hole
and separate bedrooms with locked
doors because he needs time alone
to rehearse his proper role
in this sump hole, time to remake
you into a better version of yourself.
I want to tell you there are things
you need to learn about sensitivity
and common civility. But instead,
I glance at you and see a cat
attached to your face too. And the man
who represents me during the day
pours his tea, licks his spoon, smiles,
and says, "Fine. You?"

INDEPENDENCE DAY

I wake, feel around and
remember, we've slept
in separate beds.

It's 100 degrees already.
The swamp cooler motor
screeches its angry protest

against heat and overwork.
You're in the kitchen trying
to be quiet. I hear the scrape

of a skillet, smell burnt toast.
I lie motionless, thinking
of the dry undergrowth

of love, its brittle hate,
how a match carelessly tossed
can destroy it. As I enter

you look up, tell me
fireworks are banned
this year, too dry.

Firearms too, you say.

No Netflix

They sit before a black screen.
She asks, "What movie's coming next?"
"*Elegy*," he says. "The story of a man in love
with a woman's breasts. She has to have
a double mastectomy."
She says, "I read where a seventy-year-old
woman in India had twins."
"Unnatural," he says, then adds, "The baseball
game's postponed due to rain."
She says, "I mean how many eggs
can one woman have?"
He says, "Second day in a row. Now
they have to have two double headers."
There's a long pause, then she says, "I read
that brown eggs aren't any healthier than white ones."
He says, "Puts a lot of strain on the pitching staff."
She says, "Breasts?"
He says, "Yeah, double mastectomy."
She says, "No, what's the name of the next Netflix?"
He says, "I already told you. It's *Elegy*."
She says, "This is good."
"What?" he says.
"Talking like this," she says.
He says, "Maybe we should cancel Netflix."
She says, "Want another?"
He says, "Sure."
She says, "Gin or vodka?"
"Gin," he says, "a double."
She drops some ice on the floor.
"When does *Elegy* come?" she says.

Empty Spaces

When my wife told me
she loved Jimmy, I asked
if she had sex with him.
She said, *Sort of.*
I drove north all night and thought
about what she might mean by
sort of. At noon I stopped

at a cantaloupe stand in Fallon, Nevada.
Bought a cantaloupe from the woman who
gave me her number in case
I wanted a tour later. That night
we met at a bar. Turned out
I hadn't noticed her leg brace.
I wanted to leave as soon as I saw her.
But we played shuffleboard
with another couple. Her puck kept veering
off the board because of her leg and shoulder.
I tried not to say anything, but after losing
again, I told her she'd do better if she stood
to the right and aimed farther left. She started
to cry. I took her out to my car intending

to take her home. But we talked all night.
I told her about my wife and Jimmy *sort of*
making love. She told me about having polio
when she was a kid. I'd never felt sadder
than when she asked me to touch
her steel brace. As I stroked it with my finger,
she said no one had ever done that before,
that her brace was the sturdiest thing in her life.

Next morning the interstate was empty.
No one but me and the cantaloupe I bought

from the woman with a brace. I felt around its rind
until I found a soft spot, then poked my finger
into its empty center.

A Note from Nashville

On Highway 40 west of Nashville
a sign caught my eye: *Only Five Miles*
to the Garden of Eden, and I couldn't help
thinking how tedious it would be for Adam
and Eve to spend eternity picking hibiscus
and eating persimmons with strangers.

It had to be Eve's idea, still flush from an erotic
experience with the serpent and having recently
discovered her own inner flower, poking Adam
awake and saying, *You must paint a sign.*
Chances were at this moment she was at the entrance,
her body lush in dappled sunlight, giving nervous little touches
to her hair, as she awaited her first customer.
Would it be me? I was tempted.

But I imagined Adam, brow furrowed, perplexed
that persimmons had lost their sweetness, and I guessed
he preferred the simple pleasures of occasionally
peeking out at Paradise, then retreating to more
familiar slugs and mosses. It occurred to me that,
like Adam, I have difficulty appreciating abundance
while you thrive on it. That's why I love the sparseness
of the desert, the occasional wildflower that sprouts
in the midst of nothingness. So when the next sign said,

Turn here, I thought of you bedded down with your new lover,
happy again. I kept my foot on the pedal, turned on the radio
and headed for the city of sad music, loyal dogs, and lonely hearts.

Empathy Interrupted

I trace the rim of my glass
with an attentive finger. Two hours
we've been talking about ex-spouses
and how much we miss our children.
Now she's telling me about a floor lamp
her ex-oldman stole from her and how
he ruined it painting the shade
with black enamel. I am discerning
innuendo here, detecting nuance, but lose
my concentration because in the next booth
a man and woman are arguing about ferrets.
He's saying he'll replace her goddamn ferrets
but won't pay the vet's bill. She's crying
and saying she doesn't want his replacement ferrets,
she wants her original ones. He reminds her
that her original goddamn ferrets are dead,
and she says something about ferrets
not being replaceable like engine parts.
The woman across the table is still talking
about the lampshade, measuring
my compassion over the rim
of her glass. She asks if she's
just imagining it, or is the world
totally fucked? The ferret woman
says fuck you and leaves. I try
not to blink, but those ferrets
are still in my head. I take a sip,
breathe, execute a slow nod, and say,
I know exactly how you are feeling,
and all the while I'm trying
to remember how long it's been
since I cared for anything
as much as that woman cares
for those ferrets.

The Morning After

Why did I drink it—a full pint of Old Crow
on top of a plate full of fettuccine?
And that motel with the moldy shower curtain.
So cheap.
So disgusting.
And the woman's—God, I can't even remember
her name—her chipped front tooth, her insistence
on saying "me and him."
So sleazy.
So unsophisticated.
How could anyone with sensitivity and conscience
be expected to perform under those conditions?

SWAGGERING

He stands on his tenth floor balcony and watches
four skateboarders traverse ledges, leap
over steps, slide down curved handrails.
They crash every time, but it doesn't matter.
Their reward is in their style, their swagger
after they fail.

There's a dot of blue pool below, and
a ghostly terrified part of himself leaves
the balcony, extends, executes three full
gainers, almost manages a fourth just before
he hits the water spread-eagled.

There's no laughter, no expectations, no regrets,
just an approving nod from the sad man
still standing on his balcony, the man who
has no interest in anything except those
skateboarders, the man who now crawls
over the railing, leans out and waves.

If they notice him, if they wave back,
he'll do it—something breathtaking, something
that gives him ten seconds of life. But
they don't look up. Nobody sees him,
and after a while he returns to his room, pulls
the curtain closed and sits on the bed. He wants
to call his ex-wife but doesn't. Another man
is bedding her now. Another man. He switches off
the light and imagines himself swaggering
in the face of failure.

Quitting

When the quality of Yokohama Rice Bowl's
teriyaki chicken began to seriously deteriorate,
you told me you couldn't understand why
I persisted filling out my Buy-Ten-Get-One-Free card.
I told you, I'm not a quitter. By my eighth bowl,
the rice was gummy and the chicken moldy,
but I kept going back and finally ate enough
to order my free bowl. It was even moldier

than the rest, and as I finished it, some heroic
quitters I've known came to mind—a man
who spent two thousand on a drum set,
then walked away because he hated practicing,
a woman who met a Harley guy and, against
my advice, took off cross-country. They made it
as far as Vegas before he left her at a rest stop.
A dear friend who, in the space of a year, became
a failed novelist, a not-quite-certified swimming
instructor, a former sculptor, a born-again Christian,
and an atheist. I admired their lack of tenacity,

their ability to walk away. On the whole they seemed
happier than me. But a beaver cannot become a swan.
I called you on my cell phone and told you
I'd just finished my free bowl. How was it,
you asked. Lousy, I said, but it'll be better
next time. You're crazy, you said. Don't leave,
I said. I listened to the dial tone for a full minute
before I hung up.

An Evening with My Ex-wife

We sit at opposite ends of her new sofa,
sip ouzo, and listen to her new Lena Horne
CD while rain snakes off her roof. A second
ouzo and I lie about skydiving lessons. A third
and she curls her legs under her, smoothes
her skirt, and tells me she's met an artist
who paints vipers. Her head moves in rhythm
to *Ain't Misbehavin'* while I chew an ice cube
and wonder what it would take to stop her
from moving her head like that. This artist, I ask,
which particular vipers does he paint?
Her nostrils flare just slightly, then she
stands up and says I'd better go.
A block away my car stalls. Water everywhere.
My wipers just smear things around. I stand
outside, feel the rush of water and twigs
around my ankles, look for the curb,
a fallen branch to hold onto. I check
her house just as the porch light goes off.
I stand there hardly breathing, motionless,
hoping nothing will strike.

GOLDFISH CHILDREN

Suitcase in hand, I kissed my children goodbye.
On my way to my new apartment, I bought
two goldfish and named them Jenny and Danny.
I wanted my children to see how much I loved them,
how nothing had changed. On their first weekend
visit, I showed them the fish and explained
that even when I wasn't with them, they were,
in a manner of speaking, with me. The children

made fish lips and pretended to swim around
the rug until Jenny took a closer look and said,
"Danny's dead." "Not me," Danny said. I jiggled
the bowl and said, "He's just napping." "No sir,"
Jenny said, "his gut is hanging out and he's Danny."
Danny's face soured. "Huh-uh," was all he managed.
I suggested a movie, then Dairy Queen. "I better
not be dead when we get back," Jenny said.
She wasn't and Danny bawled. Later that night

while they slept between crinkly new Mickey
and Minnie sheets just like the ones at home,
I carried the goldfish to the bathroom, locked
the door and flushed Jenny and Danny down
the toilet. And as they disappeared in a golden
swirl, I got it. My children at age four and two
knew about death, their own deaths and the death
of love between their parents. Somehow they knew

that nothing would ever be the same. Wind
that whistled through the cracks around the door
would feel colder. The cup that held their milk
wouldn't fit the hand as well. *Three Little Pigs*
would become a story of terror. The thread
that connected my children's days had been broken.
The meaning of love changed. And it would change
more and more as all the little deaths took their toll.

The Next Thing You Say

She called at two in the morning
in tears. "I must see you,"
she said. "Now. It can't wait."
I drove to the house on College Avenue,
certain she wanted to get back together,
knowing I'd agree if she asked
because I missed the kids so. And when
I arrived she was waiting in her robe
at the curb. Inside the car, she found
her breath, wiped away the tears
and said almost too simply,
"I want you to have custody."
Then came the outpouring
of reasons why, but I didn't
hear them. All I could hear
was my own inner voice screaming,
The next thing you say will be
the most important words
you've ever said in your life.
I waited until she finished and said,
"This has to be hard for you." There
were more words, more tears including
mine. My head was exploding
with joy and something dark and sinister
and unbearably sad for having been granted
a gift I'd never dreamed of having.
The children were packed and ready
to go. I carried them to the car and drove
away into a place where love is all
and knows no boundaries.

PART FOUR

ASHES, ASHES

One minute I'm watching
basketball on TV. The next
I'm rigid with fear. A camel
drools on my feet. A rabbit sits
quivering in the corner. Water flows
from every wall. Mexicans have
planted a bomb under my bed. I saw
them do it. I saw the bomb. I
beg for a gun to kill them, warn everyone,
RUN, RUN. Three nurses come
with needles. I grab wildly and find
a wrist. I can snap it. I know I can snap it.
More white coats and suddenly
we're playing a children's game,
holding hands, spinning in a circle,
lunging faster and faster until
the one who's "it" shouts,
Ashes, ashes. All fall down. We hit
the ground laughing, pointing
to the last to fall, 'cause that one's "it"
and "it" rhymes with shit. HELP ME,
someone yells as bone cracks
under my grip. I try to scream,
to force the words from my throat,
I'M NOT IT. I'M NOT IT. But
nothing except the horror of silence
comes out.

Hospice

One day a blond woman leans against my door frame
eating a hotdog. I wonder if she can see my camel
and the water. She wipes mustard from her mouth,
walks to my bed and holds my hand. Her eyes glisten
with tears. I tell her she has mustard on the back
of her hand. She asks if I want to lick it off. I lick
like a lion that's made a fresh kill. When I finish,
she pulls back my covers, lies by my side and kisses me,
a soft lingering wet kiss. I smell mustard, feel its pungent
sting on my tongue. I close my eyes and when I open
them, she's gone. I search my hand for a sign,
a yellow stain. Nothing's there. I believe I'm dead.

Then a doctor explodes into the room—stethoscope,
pushing, probing, asking questions I can't understand.
I ask about the woman in white, the hotdog. I ask
if I'm dead. *You're not dead,* he says. *We're transferring
you to another unit.* The room is suddenly dark.
I'm not dead, I whisper. *I'm not dead…*An attendant
appears with applesauce, yogurt, peas, meatloaf. *Anything
you need?* he says. *Mustard,* I say. *Do you have any mustard?*

Afraid of Death

I worry that people who die are forgotten, that
my children will remember a few Papa stories,
that their children will see me forever as the one
in the photo who's dressed like a gorilla. I worry
that their children will know me, if at all,
as a remote hollow square on a genealogical tree.

I worry about poetry I want read at my memorial and
who will spread my ashes. I worry about the people
who might be present to honor my demise. No, present
is not enough. I want *fully* present people, faces twisted
with suffering. I think about what I might do to attract
more and sadder people. I'm concerned about not believing

in an afterlife. I've tried unsuccessfully to stop questioning
the aesthetics of people who dream up places like heaven
and hell. I don't want to spend eternity surrounded
by bad taste. I've tried prayer and looked for signs—a small
burning bush, a lost sock suddenly appearing, the face
of the Virgin Mary imbedded in my morning toast.

What I really want is my friends, a room that smells
of cedar, some Lena Horne CDs, my favorite books,
the sun, a snowfall now and then, a notebook, my orange
cup filled with sharpened pencils, a way to make coffee.
Come to think of it, what I really want for all eternity
is something close to what I have now.

Last to Go

I arrived strapped to a wheelchair,
diagnosed (misdiagnosed it turned out)
with Lewi Body—a form of Alzheimer's
with rapid brain cell deterioration, a rapid
descent into a paranoid hell, and sadly,
no quick death, only the endless inner clang
of metal sunsets tolling permanent separation
from the species.

My first breakfast—eight women with tattered
palm tree hair, three men beyond despair
locked inside boxes of silence, and me,
not yet silenced, afraid and confused.
Not the usual juice and cereal, but *bacon*,
the nurse said in such a happy tone
that bacon must surely be the gold ring
of our Alzheimer's merry-go-round. Bacon
squirreled away in bulging jowls, bacon
in robe pockets, a crisp piece shoved
into a wrinkled bra. This is the last to go,
I thought—the opium high of bacon.

That evening six women slowly encircled
me in their wheelchairs, some with combed hair,
some with wigs. Robes exchanged for dresses,
polished nails, rouged cheeks, painted lips.
Twelve empty hands, fingers dancing as if crocheting
or picking petals from flowers, or saying the rosary.
Six smiles shaped like hawk wings caught
in an updraft. Six worn-out gardeners come
to cultivate the weeds of me until I burst
into blossom. Little nursery rhymes of hope—
*touch me, touch you, love, make love,
my room, please come, oh, please come my love*

I wedged my way through their metal web
and fled. One who smelled of smoldering driftwood
wheeled behind me—arms outstretched, elbows
holding off the attendant, calling: *I love him. He's
my husband. He's come to take me golfing.*
The attendant rolled her away, shaking his head
with sighs of resignation. I never saw her again

but her cries echoed in my head. That night
I awoke and, in a moment of clarity, I knew
that the last brain cells to go have tendrils
rooted in the heart that cling to every beat
and fight to the last to give and receive love.

Making a Deal with God

God, you have to understand.
For a while I really believed
I'd been chosen, convinced
myself that I was an angel
of some kind. My ecstatic insights
terrified and astonished me.
I loved everyone and everything,
toads and sand and bark on trees.
I loved garbage and thought
I understood suffering. Then suddenly
these insights vanished like a flock of pigeons.

For a while I faked it—lifted lines
from Gibran, Mother Theresa
and Moses. But I came to suspect
they faked it too. Gibran died bitter
and disillusioned. Mother Theresa,
racked with doubt, faked her faith
all those years. And I suspect all that
loving your neighbor and *not coveting
other's wives* wasn't really Yours,
just the delusions of a demented
old man who had no teeth and still
liked to bite. You see, I understand.

The unknowable is Your realm,
and You get upset when we humans
dare to think we know and comprehend
anything. I understand. A kind of earned
ignorance is the best we can hope for,
not stupidity, just a kind of golden
question mark that comes after years
of trying to make sense of things.
I understand that finally embracing
the gift of not-knowing is true grace.

So I'm back to being human—doing
my laundry, eating my Cheerios, judging
others, hating most politicians, coveting
wives—the whole human disaster. God,
should you exist, even in ways that are
beyond comprehension, here's my proposal:
Grant me a few more years of being me,
and I'll stay on my side of the fence—
no more ecstatic insights, no more thinking
I actually know something. Hey, I'd be willing
to consider a counterproposal. But that's not
going to happen, is it? See, I get it.

Lazarus and Me

His body was wrapped in a sheet, you remember,
his flesh surely half-rotten, when he heard
the voice say, *Lazarus, come forth!* He couldn't

come forth of course because he was wrapped
in a sheet and his legs were weak. He, like me,
must have peered through dusty light and focused

on the group of on-lookers that shuffled forward
and told him the not-quite-believable story of his death
and resurrection. Like me, he must have checked

to see if he was sprouting wings, imagining himself
an angel sent to help others, to serve the better good.
He must have wondered if he might have a message,

if only he could find the right words to spread that message.
But at the time, religious testimonials must have seemed
trivial compared to worrying about falling off the toilet.

We both, I'm sure, had aches and pains, running sores
and dislocations that didn't appear to be healing. Did
Lazarus began to suspect he was the brunt of a practical joke?

Did he wonder why the so-called miracle worker hadn't healed
his sore leg, given him back his lost muscles, replaced
his missing tooth? Shouldn't any true worker of miracles

toss in a bonus of a little less suffering? And the biggest
question of all, *Why us?* All we can do is moan and suffer.
Why not a great singer or a talented dancer? Then one day

a thought came to me, and I suspect to Lazarus,
that maybe resurrection wasn't about salvation.
Maybe we had to learn to live with suffering.

If it's true, as the Buddhists claim, that we must learn
to endure suffering, then we need our bodies, for
bodies are the only containers we have for suffering.

And so I moved into a different realm, one where
life is a container for suffering, as well as love and joy.
I don't know how resurrection changed Lazarus' life

or how any other near-death survivors felt afterward,
but this message, this thought about suffering
is the best I can do. I guess the same goes for loving.

Exuberant Suffering

Once upon a time a leper lost the clapper he used
to warn the non-infected of his coming. So instead
of finding a new one, he decided to laugh instead
of clap. Soon other lepers followed his lead
and leper laughter echoed throughout the village.
This method of forewarning evoked profound fear
and solemnity among the villagers. And eventually
a Stop-the-Lepers-from-Laughing movement started.

Villagers gathered in houses and on street corners
to express their disgust and to demand deportation
of all laughing lepers. But when a leper happened by,
one or two weak-willed villagers couldn't help but join in
with sympathetic snickers. Thus laughter spread
from a single root to a massive tree, and before long
cows weren't milked, giggling children wandered about
without clothes. The priest found himself unable
to complete communion and denounced laughter
as a sign of demonic possession. And lepers became

even more feared and hated. However, having nothing
to lose, they continued to laugh their warnings.
Whereupon, governing elders passed a law
banning "exuberant suffering," and ruled that any
leper caught laughing would be banished to a nearby
colony. When the last of the laughing lepers
waved his goodbyes, exuberant suffering disappeared,
and groaning and silent suffering assumed its proper place.
But at night, when winds were calm and waters still, the souls
of the dying and those in great pain still resonated
to the redemptive sounds of laughing lepers.

Occupant

Home from the hospital after four months,
a stranger had moved in, a spidery old man
who looked like me, except worse—thin
beyond belief, wobbly walking stick, knotted
patches of hair. I called him Occupant, scribbled
notes for him and left them on the counter.
Dear Occupant, the first began. I wrote
about a pear on the sill that had rotted
while I was away. My second note
reflected on the symbolism of wearing adult diapers.

I'd stare at my old coffee cup, turn it this way
and that. It was not mine. I wrote a note demanding
to know what Occupant had done with my cup.
I wrote about being afraid of death and wondered
if he might have some comforting words on the subject.

I began walking, short distances at first. Then
one day foraged my way down into the thicket
of trees behind my house. The monsoons had turned
everything dark. Flowers, bent from their own weight,
strained to pull their heads from the muck. Syrupy
rivulets flowed in every direction. I lost a shoe in the mud
and sat on the trunk of a fallen tree. I was lost and afraid.

And when I looked up a soft light shone through
the twisted fingers of trees. A small bird hopped
from limb to limb as if saying, *follow me, follow me.*
I felt lost but not afraid, homeless and home again.

Soon thereafter, I stopped using my cane, combed
my hair, ate toast dripping with raw honey, and took
longer and longer walks, forcing myself to go places
I'd never been before, to get lost again and again.
One morning I placed an unripe pear, Buddha-like,

on the sill and sat for a while each day watching
the pear ripen—plump, unperturbed, happy.

The last note I wrote to Occupant was about a blue marble
I'd found on my walk, how it reflected the sun. I wrote
about ants in my kitchen, how well we all seemed to be
getting along together. I suggested the two of us might
get together and have a serious talk, but next day,
Occupant wasn't there. Maybe he never was, but
I choose to believe differently.

THE ZIPPER

Strolling is a habit now.
I walk to the park, sit on my favorite
bench and walk back. One morning
an old man in a bathrobe and slippers
was sitting in my place, looking
up at the sky. Unwilling to give up
my spot, I sat beside him and
after a while felt compelled
to look up too. I saw nothing except
blue sky. I asked if he lived nearby.
He said they let him out to see
if it's still there. "What?" I said.
He pointed to the sky. "That zipper.
You see it?" I told him I didn't and asked
if he'd ever seen camels or rabbits or water
flowing from his walls. He said he hadn't,
just the zipper. He pulled his robe tighter
and said he wished he could grow wings,
that he'd like to fly up there, unzip
that thing to see through to the other side.
I asked what he thought might be there.
"More kisses," he said. It rained
that afternoon. I sat looking out the window
at the dark sky. The scents of rain
and cherry smoke wafted through the vents.
A ruffled bird clung to a bare branch as if
staying alive was its only desire. I thought
of the man who saw the zipper and
wondered why we don't give up, why we persist
when the odds are against us, but how lucky
we are to be able to create zippers that give
hope and promises of more kisses.

Revelation

Rod, my mechanic, lingers, wipes
his hands, asks if I've had any insights
as a result of my recent near-death.
Says he's working harder than ever,
getting no place. I sense his need
for something wise and my need
not to let him down. I have no insights
to offer, but remember a book I read
days before, "Seven Sins for a Life
Worth Living." I can't remember
all seven, but I dredge up three and
a Bertrand Russell quote. So I tell him
what I remember and add a little riff
of my own after each one. "First,
don't be afraid of being foolish. Second,
it's all right to be imperfect. Third,
there's great pleasure and worth
in being ordinary." Then as an encore
I toss in the Russell quote, "One of the symptoms
of an approaching nervous breakdown
is the belief that your work is important."
Rod stares at his hands for a moment,
then looks up, eyes full. "Thanks,
he says, "I think you nailed me."
He shakes my hand. "It's been great
talking with you," he says.
I drive away feeling foolish, flawed
and ordinary. But, I confess, more
important than when I went in.

Spiritual Development

As a near-death survivor I was determined
to be a vessel of peace, a non-judgmental,
forgiving man who sees the worth
of fellow humans. I took a class
in spirtual development at the Unitarian
Church and did my best to listen, support
and value the contributions of others.
I offered no arguments, clarified others
feelings and talked about my own.

Then one week, before offering
a nigglet of critical comment, I paused
and said, "Let me self-edit. I don't want
to make anyone angry." And a classmate
said, "Dan, you make people angry
even when you self-edit." Another member
said something I can't remember but it included
pompous. A thind joined in with *loose cannon*.
Where does one go after flunking spiritual
development at the Unitarian Church?

Frankly, it was a mixed blessing. Spirituality
weighed a lot more than cannon balls. I admit
I love leading with my mouth and asking questions
later. I discover what I'm thinking when I talk,
and I sometimes delight and surprise myself
with what I say. Truth is, straining to be
spiritual, thinking before I speak and being nice
for the sake of being nice, slows my world down,
turns me into a politician and paints everything
human with a beige veneer of unfelt courtesy.

Faucet Dogs

I'm not sure how "old" feels,
but I feel old today—off balance,
joints swollen. It's mid-July hot,

and it doesn't help that there's a billboard
with a half-naked girl inviting me to scratch
my itch and strike it rich at the local

Native American casino. I know I'm not
its target market. Across the way, two old dogs
share licks from a mossy faucet, and

that gives me a kind of sad hope,
just why, I don't know. I sit on a bench,
take off a shoe and walk over to those dogs.

They wag their tails, and I toss my shoe
as far as I can. The dogs bring it back
playing tug-of-war as if my shoe's worth something.

They lick from the faucet and wait for me
to throw it again. I spend an hour
or so playing *Fetch the Shoe,* not thinking

about much, just enjoying these two beasts,
the clouds, rolling on the grass, the pretend
growling and biting, watching those dogs take

turns licking from that dripping faucet—
me, feeling like I'm a man with a purpose.

My Need to Be Seen

In bed last night we talked about death.
"I'd like to go to sleep and not wake up,"
you said. I said I might want more fanfare,
that I didn't want to be a mere sword carrier
in my death but wanted to play a leading role.

"I don't want a memorial service," you said.
I confessed I'd already scripted mine, chosen
poems, arranged seating, hired a saxophonist
to play a slow jazz version of "Bye Bye Love."
I said I'd like to be present at my memorial,
that I wanted a standing ovation as I self-delivered
with the help of drugs, vodka, and inhaling helium.

"I just want my ashes buried in the back yard,"
you said. I admitted I worried about what happens
if the saxophonist finishes before me, how embarrassing
it would be to have to lift the plastic bag from my head
and say, *One more time, please.*

"You're an exhibitionist," you said. I said, "That's
the only way to get noticed in this world."

"Why do you need to be noticed when celebrities
and you all end up at the same place?" you said.

That stopped me. I couldn't think of anything to say.
You kissed me and turned out the light. I lay awake
worrying about my need to be seen, to be the center
of attention. I listened to your breathing and for no reason
I knew, my eyes welled. I listened to your steady breaths
and thought of oars dipping into a still lake. I synchronized
my breathing with yours and together we rowed
into the deeper waters of sleep.

PART FIVE

All of Us

shuffle forward toward a gate,
two-by-two in a line as far
as the eye can see. I think of cattle,
the steel ball that enters the head,
their knees buckling. The man in front
of me is crying. I want him to stop,
but figure he has a right. Ahead
of him a blind woman taps her cane.
A child walks next to me. There are
enough animals to fill a fleet of arks.
Fishes and birds, insects and rodents.
A man in a suit studies the Journal
still trying to figure out what to buy
and what to sell. A beggar asks for a cigarette.
The Pope is there, royalty from every nation,
famous actresses and actors, heroes and villains.
A muffled snicker. A scream. A shout,
PRAISE GOD. Then only the sound
of shuffling feet. All of us together, shuffling
in step, afraid but past being depressed.
We shuffle forward, this infinite chain
of bewildered souls who no longer chase time.
The child's hand touches mine as if to say,
this is my last chance for love. I hold his
hand and reach for another's.

Missing Parts

As I write this JoAn is having a nose job,
not the ski slope kind rich folks get,
but one to remove a cancer. We went out
yesterday, broke every rule we knew
about healthy eating, saw Mickey Rourke's
mutilated and juiced-up body make its comeback
in "The Wrestler." Too bloody for JoAn,
too religious for me. I mean, at the risk
of giving the ending away, Rourke dies,
not for our sins but his. After the movie,

we ate Greek food and I couldn't help staring
at her nose, trying to imagine her looking
okay without it. She joked about putting
a band aid across the holes. I dipped
a wedge of pita in hummus and gave
her idea serious thought. I was ashamed
that this seemed so important to me. So
I told her I wouldn't mind a missing
breast or two, but I wasn't sure about a nose.
I told her a missing nose might affect
how often we went to the movies.

I'm waiting at home now, thinking
about the cruelties of life and waiting
for her to walk in the door. Kitty's waiting too,
sleeping on my arm rest. Kitty has a strange
at-onement with the world, prefers sleeping
to worrying about mutilation, really doesn't
care if JoAn shows up with a nose or not.
I stroke her between the ears, trying to take in
a little of what she's got, and I think about
my own missing part, the part of me that
could love a good woman with a missing nose.

Unfinished Brownies

5:00 a.m. 53 degrees, clear.
Tucson sleeps after surviving
another night of the rapes and random
shootings too many of us have come
to take for granted. In my underwear,
I stand at the sink pushing down
a handful of pills with a can of V-8.
JoAn sleeps curled around Kitty,
her gifts for living still intact
after an unnamed illness made
a playground of her heart, lungs,
and spinal column.

Last night after dinner, determined
to get better, she announced she'd make
brownies, that we'd drink milk and eat
the whole panful. But she grew weak
and had to go back to bed. The flour,
chocolate and sugar wait on the counter,
abandoned like an artist's model
for an unfinished still life

I glance through the morning paper.
The same old stuff—someone's tinkering
with voting machines, an evangelical
is caught bedding his lover, yet another
car bombing in Iraq, Vonnegut died.
Vonnegut died! I feel the sharp jerk
of a choke chain. I want to fix things,
stop all this suffering. But all I can do
is finish these brownies and eat them
in bed with JoAn. Then we'll wait and see.
Wait and see. I mix the butter with
the sugar and try to remember that famous
Vonnegut line. *And so it goes.* I add flour
and eggs. *And so it goes. And so it goes.*

One Night Stand with the Muse

Four a.m. Across the hall you're sleeping.
Wind taps a bush branch against my window.
I'm in my office cuddled with the muse.

She has finally kept our date. She kisses
my cheek, strokes my brow. I write, *Soft
wind plants a perfect kiss.* It feels adulterous.

No time. I suck her fecund breast and picture
you hugging your pillow, the same wind winding
its way into your dreams. I write, *Another day slashes*

*open the clouds, peeks through to announce it's time.
I think of yellow daisies turning to flour, the rasp
of dried leaves underfoot.* God, this is good.

I've waited so long. Now she's here
guiding my pen—amazing lines, astonishing
stanzas—anticipating the surprise ending

that takes me to a place I've never been before.
But wait. In the distance a skillet scrapes
across the burner. The aroma of coffee, bacon

and scrambled eggs infuse the air. I write, *Will
I ever know what I most desire, what I wish most
to know, where the soul wants to be?* The smell

of bacon is overwhelming. I put my pen down,
close my notebook, tell the muse I love her
and assure her this has never happened to me before.

Then I walk to the kitchen, see your body that contains
that slept-in look and puffy smile, the hand that holds
the skillet filled with your plump morning burritos.

GOOD KITTY

Monday: I decide to become the steward
of my own health, eat life-giving foods,
watch less cheerleading competition on TV,
stop fretting about cripples getting the good parking,
meditate, brush my cat, begin each day
repeating an affirmation about my own decency.
For lunch I eat a modest portion of non-fat
cottage cheese and a few raw almonds.

Tuesday: I drink half a bottle of Trader Joe's wine,
eat a whole macaroni and cheese casserole,
watch re-runs of Wheel of Fortune. Hate
the pale, wobbly slob I see reflected in the TV screen,
hate my flat toothpaste, hate my cat for her lack
of goals, her all-too-casual approach to life,
her commitment to nothing except strokes,
nibbles, and goat cheese.

Wednesday: I try to train Kitty to sit up
and meow for food. She can't make the connection.
So I order her to do what she's doing—lie down,
purr, lick her paws, yawn, eat. "Good Kitty."
Her lids slowly sink. "Sleep," I demand,
and she sleeps. I turn off the TV, eat
some non-fat cottage cheese, drink a martini,
stroke my smart cat, feel almost holy.

UGLY THINGS

Half crazy from lack of sleep, I sit
at the kitchen counter at 2:23 reading
a poem by Anne Sexton called *Cockroach.*
As I read, a real one appears as if summoned.
It pauses next to my glass of milk and looks up
to ask, *What are you doing in my night world?*
Repulsed, I try to smash it, but I'm no match
for its agility and speed as it darts beneath
my toaster and vanishes.

I wait, besieged by disgust, visions of filth.
Killing this roach becomes a cause for destroying
the ugliness in this tired world and in me.
Finally it skitters from beneath the toaster,
darts across the counter, stops and looks up.
I hear it say, *If you think you've got problems,*
try walking in my shoes, living on crumbs,
everyone trying to kill you. I raise my book,
but can't smash it. The roach seems so alert,
so single-minded, so intent on survival.

I read Sexton's poem aloud. It's a poem
of consolation for the roach's low status.
When I come to two lines near the end, I stop.
I inhale and read the lines again.
Yet I know you are only the common angel
turned into, by way of enchantment, the ugliest.
Together we silently consider this possibility.
Then the roach turns and zips back to my toaster.
For some reason I close my eyes and force myself
to feel my way back to my bed. Certain I'm
being watched, I lie awake, alert, listening
to the din and hum of ugly angels at work.

The Yawn of Life

Kitty's curled in my lap,
paws crossed, eyes closed,
head turned almost to the ceiling.

I'm reading a book but the words
are hazy and meaningless.
Outside, a light rain falls

onto oak leaves that spill
water into mouths of thirsty
flowers and you come yawning

into the room, eyes to floor,
open the refrigerator and bend over
for something on the bottom shelf.

Interest stirring, I become the rain
and you become the flower. You turn
your head and manage a smile.

It's these moments, these particular
intersections of time and life
when good things come together

in the contented yawn of life,
a time when we close our books
and glimpse the reason for living.

BLESS RAYMOND CARVER

At the annual Friends of the Library sale
I found a hard cover copy of *A New Path
to the Waterfall* marked with a big yellow *R*,
his last book, poems written when his feet
had gone numb and his lungs were covered
with tumors too numerous to count.

I opened it to the last page and felt
his presence, the faint scent of leather
and tobacco, the lapping of water
against a bow, the lazy flap of a
sail, his voice, barely audible,
nothing left but a whisper.

I owned a copy already but bought
this one anyway. It cost a dollar and
when the woman who took my money
kidded me about being a big spender,
I asked if she had ever heard of Raymond Carver.
She said she didn't believe she had,
so I opened the book to the last page.
Listen to this, I said:

*And did you get what
you wanted from this life, even so?
I did.
And what did you want?
To call myself beloved, to feel myself
beloved on the earth.*

That's lovely, she said. Is he still living?
Oh, yes, I said. More than most.

No More Knowledge Please

I stand before dusty books and
pass a finger over their spines.
I'm grateful their promises
will never be fulfilled, pleased
that this lack of information
will leave more room for imagination.
For it's the ignorance of passion I crave now.
Of course it invites superstition,
paganism, empty ritual. But I want
the bones of the world boiled
until I'm free of knowing. No more
all-you-can-eat buffets of knowledge.
No more synthesizing and memorizing.
Down with Google. No more
frantic searches for solutions. No more
gurus and their clichés. No more sophistry
to correct my wrong thinking. Smaller
portions please, a page here,
a sentence there, an occasional
morsel of fact, but just one,
and not too often. I crave
the nights of artists and soothsayers.
No more knowledge please. I commit
body and soul to protecting the small
burrowing night animal called imagination.

OLD MAN, YOUNG MAN

The old potter's wheel is now
motor driven, but his heels
still kick in rhythm
to its whirls as clay pours
forth from his flesh. He doesn't
look up, wanting to believe
his world is enough, but
through the opaque film
of his eyes he sees
the young man holding
his hands to task, feels
his youth's unspoken
words of praise gather
on his dry tongue
as his bent fingers form
the pot's lip and slurry
the surface smooth.
Here in his deep valley of age,
two hearts beat as one.
Two souls play in the same mud.

AND COOK

At times I'm a miser, afraid to offer
even a crumb of this imperfect thing
called my love. How silly my love
will seem, how tiny and insignificant.

But now as you sit at the counter, sip
your wine and watch my every move
as I cook, I'm prone to preen and canter
about. And when I show you my baked

chicken with its golden skin, scent
of garlic and sun-ripe lemons picked
from my own tree, when you roll
happy eyes, laugh and applaud,

I proclaim I will amaze you.
I will carve a hole in my chest
and release the white doves
trapped in my heart. After eating

we linger, candlelight dancing
on your greasy lips that received
my chicken in great hungry
mouthfuls and washed it down

with gulps of amber wine. I look
at you and see a home long forgotten.
I'm helpless, a featherless sparrow
fallen into your nest of love.

SAYING GOODBYE

It pre-deceased me, died a good death I suppose,
one brought on by cracks and strains of old age.
The plumber and I stood in the hall with the detached

toilet between us. I think he sensed my grief, for
he suggested I could use it as a planter or
an umbrella stand. He was a big but gentle man.

Clearly, he'd been through separation grief before.
Or I could just take it away, he said. Where?
I asked. He said we probably shouldn't talk
about that. I considered his suggestions.
My toilet had lived a long and useful life. It
was born with one idea and expressed

that idea perfectly for thirty years. Oh,
that I were so determined, so resilient.
To turn it into a flower pot would violate

its nature. I imagined a graveyard for toilets,
thousands of them stacked high, mine on top,
its porcelain gleaming in the sun. Take it, I said.

GRAVITY

You're sitting on the edge
of the bed now, naked, applying
lotion to your body, and a tune
is running through my head:
London Bridge is falling down,
falling down, falling down.
London Bridge is falling down,
My fair lady.

You pull on your pantyhose while
I watch but dare not tell you
that the part I don't get is *My fair lady.*
Is it *her* actual bridge that's falling,
and if so, is she losing it by some travesty?
Or is gravity the culprit here? Could be
her bridge is simply old and tumbling
of its own accord. You stretch the nylon

over one leg, then the other and wiggle
into the crotch the way you do,
and, still braless, you turn and ask,
"Aren't you getting ready?"
I'm taken aback by the urgency
in your voice, and suddenly I see
that the falling bridge is a metaphor—
the poet's way of celebrating
the years of pleasure his *fair lady's*
bottom and bodice have given him,
and it occurs to me that gravity
is the expression of the earth's
yearning to reclaim its own flesh. So I say,

"You look fantastic. Come here."
And you do. You fall into my arms.

Fading Memories

I can't remember the color of the dress you wore,
the one that lifted to receive the wind when we sat
on the cliff in Mexico. I remember your eyes,
how they reflected the sunset, but I can't remember

if they were blue or hazel. Even your face has faded.
And what was the name of the wine we drank
before our first kiss? That's gone forever. And what
did we have for dinner that night? I can't even remember

who placed my hand on your breast. Was it you?
I must have made it up the next morning. Nothing
could be that beautiful. Did the sun burst from the night
like light from lemons? The sweetest memories lie hidden

in tunnels of imagination. I'd like to remember exactly
the invasion of your hungry lips, the smooth firmness
of your breasts, but that is gone forever. Perhaps the love
I feel from your reflected light is even better.

COFFEE SHOP WRITERS

Many are at it today.
Most use a computer
to copy notes from books.
But a girl at the window writes
with a number two pencil
on a yellow pad, no books,
just the age-old act of unraveling
strings of memories and visions
and assigning them to the page
and thus, to all of us. I'm reminded
how our distant cousins used stones
by crackling fires to chip away
at the walls of their caves. The girl
is half the age of my daughter,
and I silently cheer her on with a love
I sometimes feel for people
I don't know and never will.
I wish her well because she will suffer
more than she knows and grow old.
But not now, not today. Today
she will change the world.
She pauses, sips her coffee, crosses
and recrosses her legs, gazes out
at the rush of passing cars that
could be stampeding bison
or a shower of stars. Her pencil
eraser rests on her lower lip. I send
an image: *a lioness awaiting her feeding.*
She sucks in air with a swell of pleasure
and begins to write again. Her pencil
becomes a tool used to chip away
at her imagination. As it rushes
across the page, creating words,
I hear the sound of spilled diamonds.
I finish my coffee and leave,
my work done for the day.

Sports Writing

What a remarkable gift those
sportswriters have who can write
the story of a game as it happens.
I wonder if they're prone
to seeing their days this way—
if they spontaneously characterize
a successful walk, the petting
of their cat, the taste of their
favorite wine, the whirr of a hairdryer.

This is a job I could handle,
a person hired to report the game
going on in the small stadium
of my existence—JoAn's soft grunts
as she exercises with an oversized
purple rubber band, me picking up
my crumpled red baseball cap now lying
like road kill in the corner, the breeze
through my open window, how it kisses
my skin and causes the vertical slats
to tremble like an expectant lover.

I would write about the texture
of cantaloupe I'm about to eat,
the shivering relief of urinating
this morning, the unsolvable mystery
of loving and being loved. At the end
of the day, I'd add a cliché or two,
encapsulating what was won and lost,
summarizing the highs and lows, adding
if possible, one final line of how this
relates to the larger picture. Then I'd
place my stories, one by one, atop
a precarious pile of stories that

over the years has grown tall as a Sequoia
and like that beautiful tree will not die
but fall from its own weight.

BLESS MY BROTHER

For some reason I sent a copy of my book
to my brother. I didn't know him that well.

He was eighteen years older, had Alzheimer's,
voted for Wallace and Nixon, heavy drinker,

prided himself on never reading a book because
Rush Limbaugh was enough. We were never close,

but I wanted to give and receive a few kind words
before he died. Heard nothing for three months, then

my nephew called to tell me my brother had died.
"Alzheimer's turned him to stone," he said. "Couldn't

recognize himself in a mirror." We talked but our words
were clunky and disconnected. Then just before hanging up,

he said, "Oh, I almost forgot. You know that book
you sent him? Well, during the last weeks, I read him

that poem of yours, the one about you and Gramps
watching wrestling from outside the TV store. Remember

that one? Well, every time I read it to him he smiled.
It was like watching a slab of cement come to life.

That poem of yours was the only thing that got to him."
Later I read the poem and tried to imagine what made

my brother smile. Then I tried to write something for him,
but all I got was this: *Think of these lines as bars on a window.*
On the other side there's a TV, my brother's stone face on the screen.

I'm outside. I reach through the bars, strain to touch him, stretch
as far as I can but can't quite touch the screen.

FOR BOBBY SHECHTMAN

Bobby grew art like crabgrass, found it
in grease pits, blues joints, sounds he made gargling,
the melodies tires hummed on asphalt.
He wrote a symphony for fifty cars and pickups.
I know because I played first Toyota. We brought
the house down with our slammed doors,
diverse horns, revved engines and whispering wipers.

Bobby wrote a death opera—bulls with hard-ons chasing
naked girls singing help/help arias, his barber sang tenor
while barbecuing flank steak. Everybody died happy,
doing exactly what they always wanted to do, but

Bobby died alone sleeping in his own bed. Sad for those
who knew him because we weren't there to play kazoos,
rev engines, or twist the little knobs that caused
wipers to whisper, because we weren't there to cheer him,
tell him thanks for making this world a more interesting place,
for including us, for teaching us there's no such thing
as failure because all of it can be turned into art. Now
we hear him when we turn on our worn-out wipers, hear
him whispering about the ugly things we used to hide beauty.

SUSHI

In the kitchen I'm eating leftover sushi
and listening to Mann and Shank play
tunes from *My Fair Lady*, and like
Professor Higgins, I'm thinking
wouldn't it be nice if everyone
was more like me. There'd be no art
left unappreciated, no cruelty,
no critics, not even a need for grief.

I tap my foot to Mann's driving beat,
take my last bite of sushi, pungent
with ginger and soy, and I think,
what about sushi? I'd love to keep eating it
but have no interest in making it,
so I'll have to keep a few sushi masters
around. And while I'm at it,

we'll need more buttery Julia Childs
to get through the century. Shank delivers
a soaring climax to "The Rain in Spain,"
and I decide we'll need more Shanks
and Manns, too. More Bachs and Vivaldis,
a Beckett or two to nudge us in the side
and ask us why we're waiting and just
what we intend to do. Mann pounds

his bass, crashes his cymbals and ends
with an ascending sweep of celestial
chimes. The air smells like the sea,
and I imagine a great tapestry of life
held together by the webs and knots
of every living thing extending from
the beginning forward to the unknowable.
I eat the last grains of rice, grateful for sushi
and for everyone and everything I'm not.

FOREVER

Sorting books, deciding
which to keep, which to toss,
I found a gift certificate
to a bookstore closed
twenty years ago,
signed: *Love Forever.*

She'd died shortly
afterward, still carrying
the joys and burdens
of our secret. For thirty years, she
lived two lives, one as wife and
mother of two fine children,
another as a passionate and ready
mistress of a devoted lover.

I considered throwing it away, it
and the book that held it, a book
that explored hopes of a man
and woman in love trying
to discover a less selfish path
through the jungle of secrecy.

But forever hadn't come.
I wasn't ready for those
memories to leave. I placed
the certificate back in the book
and the book back on the shelf—
there they will remain forever,
a book unread, a gift unclaimed.

PART SIX

FOOLING AROUND AFTER POETRY CLASS

After we spend two hours bailing out
the sinking dinghies of our poems, lashed
about by rip tides of criticism prefaced
by so-called *good things*, like "I love
the way you end your lines with
prepositions," we manage somehow
to reach land and sit together afterward
in the student union, drink coffee, mend tears
in our delicate poetic skins. Sitting there next

to mindless vending machines engaged
in parallel talk is like a walk through
a valley of wildflower thoughts sprung up
after a two-hour storm, a valley with no
preferences for yellow buds of delight,
or poetic reflections on our mother's red
dress or our neon-purple agonies of lost love.
And even though we may stumble across
occasional stalks of ponderous insights,
we stomp our way through these bothersome
weeds with no pause to reflect on how
they might change the world.

And on my way home I think how pleasant
all this has been, how my inner artist needs
my thick-skinned fool. For my fool frees
my artist from obsessing too much about
compressing life's horrors or finding new ways
to say, *I don't love you anymore.* It's my fool
who helps me continue to believe that next week's poem
will evoke tears of appreciation and a standing ovation.

For JoAn

When I'm mired again
on the great questions,
you keep moving forward,
doing what needs to be done,
planting roses and raking leaves.

It's this that touches me deepest,
this steadiness of course,
this strength of yours not to veer
from the grace of duty.

I remember being lost
as a child and the joy
I felt when I knew where I was.
You give me the same joy every day.

Your love is like a familiar street,
feeling the certainty of your hand
leading me to a place where
the world's suffering
becomes, for a while at least,
vaguely boring and unimportant.

What I Didn't Say

As a man who stays inside a lot
I'm always surprised when spring
comes and your flower garden
is suddenly alive, how you laugh
more and wear brighter colors.

This morning from the kitchen
window, I watched you work
the soil, watched the light that shone through
olive leaves form delicate
shadows on your face. I closed
my eyes and, for some reason, thought
of our deaths—mine and yours—how
this life we've patched together,
these flowers and even this tremulous
fear will die with us. You swept

the patio, pinched a few dead
leaves, and came inside. I must have
looked at you funny because
you smiled and asked, "What?"
"Nothing," I said, but that wasn't true.
You see, what I wanted to say,
the exact thing I wanted to say
and didn't was, Thank you.

The Future

You with your bowl of microwave
oatmeal, me with coffee and newspaper,
reminding myself not to dwell on how
and when terrorists will strike next,
who'll win the presidential election,
not to obsess over the declining market.
I watch you add sugar and tell myself
I am a man with an eye to the future,
a man alive with anticipation and hope.
But I've heard all that before. I have
become capable of boring myself.

From where I sit, I can see the neighbor's cat
shitting in our flower garden. So what,
I tell myself. Half-full, half-empty, it's the size
of the glass that counts, and mine is gigantic.
But I've heard all that before too.

You take your first bite and look up at me,
a look I've known for twenty years, a look
that reminds me how gracefully you manage
to put one foot in front of the other, unconcerned
that the future limps toward us like an old man,
that I seem to be losing my eagerness, that hope
has faded. The neighbor's cat covers its offering,

sniffs, paws once at a rose, yawns,
eyes a dove on the wall, licks its paw, washes
its face. Stretches. I read an article about a pitcher
throwing another shutout. You finish your oatmeal
and ask if there's anything interesting in the paper.
"Nothing," I say. The dove is joined by another.
The cat watches them until they both fly away.

For Quin

Four years old, twin pony tails
bouncing, she's eating licorice
when pink tutus emerge from the darkness,

then barefoot bears, a rat king, wooden
soldiers. When the number ends she shouts,
"More, I want more." When she asks

if she can dance, her mother says,
"Of course, but you must wait until
you're five." She sits motionless

waiting with no worries about
boyfriends, her worthiness,
or what others will think, buoyed

by her boat of enchantment
that is sailing smoothly
into her future.

SOME WORDS ABOUT LOVE
(for Amanda and Danny's wedding, July 11, 2009)

There are a thousand ways to kneel
and kiss the ground
                                   — Rumi

For days now I've been staring out
my window trying to think of something
I know for sure about love. Not much.
For every thing that seems certain,
the opposite seems equally true. I don't
even know what those words *I love you*
mean. The longer I think about them
the more hollow they seem. One thing
that feels true is, love lies in the particulars,
a constellation of specific acts
accumulated over a life. Love *is*
the thousand ways we kneel
every day and kiss the ground.

Remember, Danny, when you were three,
the loose change you found under sofa pillows?
I put it there. Remember the only time
I spanked you, how you didn't shed a tear?
Well, I did. I bawled my eyes out. Remember
my hesitancy to ask you to fix a meal at home
long after your culinary skills were well-honed?
That pot roast was the best I've ever tasted. And
I still laugh about the day you got fed up
when Oscar, our dog, always rested his head
in your sister's lap and you finally said,
"Why do I always get the rear?" Now you
and Amanda have Osa. She's yours, the rear, middle
and head of her—the whole dog. Add to these
your funny stories, the joy you feel with nature,
animals and children, the tremulous lost days,

your persistence until you found your path to happiness.
These and more contain the particulars of the love
I feel for you.

And Amanda, you planted the seeds of love
deep in our hearts when you sent sweets
you'd made yourself, teas and a lavender
pillow for JoAn's neck. You made me swell
with pride by asking for a list of my favorite books.
I heard the strength of your love when you
called about Danny's health and said you
loved him even more. Your foot-by-foot tour
of your back yard and your dreams was filled
with grace and certainty. And when I saw
the note you made on your kitchen
calendar under July 11, the simple declaration—
Getting Married!—it was as if Aphrodite,
with all her powers to inspire love, had guided your hand.

So, Danny and Amanda, all I can say is,
honor every form your love takes. In some way
embrace it anew each day. And as the years pass
and life demands more, remember the times
you talked from the heart, the sacrament
of preparing a meal together, the spats
that became rituals, the bolts of happiness
that stunned you senseless. Take hungry bites
from every crispy-sweet moment, for these
will become the stories that will sustain you
in your darkest hours. And through the years
remember the thousand ways you love,
and invent ten thousand more.

TURF CLUB, RENO

Forty years later I drove
down Commercial Avenue
to see if it still existed—cigar
smoking old men in plaid sports
jackets holding handicap sheets
and spoons, bent over heavy
bowls of thick oyster stew
with little six-sided crackers
and a dash of Tabasco,
everyone talking all at once
about Saratoga, Del Mar and
the triple crown. Tough, no nonsense
waitresses, smells of pot roast,
corned beef with mustard on rye,
French fries, grilled burgers, fried
onions, money, cigars. I'd eaten there
every morning at five a.m. for four years,
walked there after my night shift
at the Chapel of the Bells where
I married seventy couples a week
interested in making a different
kind of wager. All the happiness
of over fifteen thousand marriages
could not replace one single oyster,
not one cigar-chewing regular
who was placing his two dollar bet
on a race run in Australia. But
it wasn't there, nothing but a hole
in the wall, a few bare red bricks,
some broken wine bottles. I made
my way to the place where I usually sat,
stood still for a moment wishing
I believed in ghosts. A pigeon landed
nearby, probably hoping for a handout.
I understood. I was looking for one too.

OLD LOVE

We held the fire close,
danced in its flames.
Life stretched far enough
to harvest ten thousand stars.

Now we lie together
listening to the house
creak and moan. Still,
when I touch you,

some light flickers.
Is it ours or a dying star's?
You kiss the tips of my fingers.
It doesn't matter, you say.

We spoon tighter and watch
the cool moon rising. We know
our old love plays a new song each day,
preparing for a song only death can sing.

For Patricia and Roy

In this rapt moment before sleep,
in that haunting silence that comes
with evening rain, you pull him closer

and rest your hand on his back.
Your breath moth-wings on his neck
and he says he likes it when you touch him.

The moon peeks in from the window's
dark corner, and as you stare at the rivulets
on the pane, it seems important to understand,

to discover order and purpose there, signs
of courage, even helplessness as they intersect,
stop, dart left and right, arrive and disappear.

But you find nothing—no significance,
not a hint of forethought, no rhyme,
no reason why rain falls here and not there,

why you can feel so much bliss one moment
and be terrified and alone the next, by what
miracle the noise in us becomes song,

why, when we learn to dance, we can't stop leaping?
And why we die, mid-leap. It seems so perfectly imperfect—
this moment when we taste the bread and wine

of ourselves, when we receive
the blessing of not knowing just before
we join the soft waters of sleep.

This Life We've Shared

We don't talk about politics and art
much anymore, spend more time ruminating
about the aches that have wormed their way
through our bodies so long we've named them.
I'll ask about Anita, and you'll say, *Moved*
from my leg to my neck last night. You'll
ask about Arnie and I'll say, *Taken up residency*
in my left foot. We laugh and cry more.

Time has gone berserk. We sleep days
and lie awake nights, thoughts flying
like sparks from a welder's torch.
Our prairie dog birthdays pop their heads up
at irregular intervals and yodel. Often
I find myself saying things that astound me,
wise things, insights edging on the divine,
only to realize you have fallen asleep.

But this morning when I walked into the kitchen
and saw you drinking coffee and reading
the sports page, when you stood and held out
your arms, I felt like a traveler just returned
home. And when my lips touched your neck
and shoulders, an undertow of laughter
and heartache pulled me back through
the years we've shared and hurled me
forward into that thin slice of time
left together. And so help me God,
(listen, you must hear this), I'm happier now
than I've ever been. Happy that we are still
swimming as fast as we can, side by side,
in this deepening sea of love.

BLIND ARTISTS

Why is it that we reach for the highest fruit?
Why does a one-legged man run a marathon?
What is this foolishness that drives us to become
what we're not and can never be?

Are we all blind artists? Isn't our imagination
at play here, creating ourselves, our victories,
our fantasies of family, our lovers, endowing
our children with amazing looks and talents?

Are we blind artists who know the blessing
of hands moved not by thought but longing?
Don't we secretly know that our paintings become
impossible when we know what we're trying to paint?

Isn't the shadowy illusion that contains our lives
the only container for soul? Isn't blind but decisive
action the architect of a deeply lived life? Isn't it
uplifting to know that crude and incomplete

approximations are our final reward? So paint
with unseen colors. Paint with quick, broad strokes
imagining that what you are is on the canvas. Paint wildly,
without recognition. Paint fully in love with the imagined self.

For Those Who Saw Me and Let Me See Them

I want you to remember how it was when we talked.
I mean we talked in ways I've never talked before.
Often I got the feeling that we were riding a carousel,
galloping along next to one another, circling the calliope,
the rat-ta-tat-tat of the snare drum, the booming bass drum,
the tinny organ grinder rendition of "Tiptoe through the Tulips,"
and we were hearing and seeing it all from every direction.
I think we were masters at circling ideas and pieces of the world,
at seeing life from every possible angle. How liberating

that was for me, my dear one. Even when we talked about
the importance of salt or the intelligence of cockroaches,
we seemed to be always circling, seeing it all 360 degrees.
But more importantly, we were at the same time circling
one another, seeing and hearing one another. I had this feeling
of being opened, and I felt gratitude for your curious eye,
your willingness not to turn away, for you, my dear, have never

turned away, and I can't imagine a gift more precious
than being set free by being seen. After one of our talks—
about anything, our favorite movies or books or what we had
for breakfast—I always felt known, as if I'd spent some time
at the center of your universe, as if you knew me better
than any other human being, that there was nothing
about me I needed to hide or that would shock you. I felt complete,

perhaps like one of Rodin's sculptures when he finally
put his hammer and chisel down, stood back, circled around
his work and heard its inner voice say, "I'm done now. You
have finished me. Have a glass of wine. Rejoice in my completion."
With you, dear one, I know I've been seen and accepted.
I know I've been completed by your eyes. So I say to you,
your work is complete. You have allowed me to exist
in three dimensions. Sit with your memories of me for a while,
have a glass of wine and give me your eyes as if I'm your finest work.

Hummingbird
(for Roy)

In morning light
he watches the hummingbird on the patio.
It's teaching him how to stand still.
He's watched for an hour admiring
its colors, how it stays in one place,
still, yet so passionate.

He glances down
at his old slippers, eats what's left
of the popcorn he and his love shared
last night. Nothing to be conquered.
No ambition. Just a softness
of spirit, the kind that seeps
over the edge when the glass is full.

He listens to his neighbor's
barking dog who is accompanied
this morning by Mozart, up early
performing across the street.

He breathes in the scent
of the orange on the counter,
remembers his love still sleeping
in tangled sheets, how their hands,
like roots, seem to find a way
to comforting places.

There are the juice glasses
they used for wine, the dried cork
still standing. He sits in this place,
in this particular light, hovering
over this blooming flower called
his life, still like a hummingbird

in this place where other lives
meet like water and flow into him,
and him into them.

You Asked What I Wanted You
to Remember About Me

I said, *everything*. Don't leave out anything.
Remember every shoelace that came untied,
my missionary work in Brazil, every puerile
whisper, every peck on the cheek. Remember
every loose-lipped, mouth-gaping, tongue-probing kiss,
every slap on your ass as the sound of a great
sexual drum marching us off that great cliff-diving
leap into the ocean of orgasm. Remember every
poem we ever read together, the cricket with the
broken back in the motel in Elko, the wounded elk
in Yellowstone who pleaded for its life, the Koi
we fed in Japan, the time I skydived onto the crest
of Mount Everest and saved twenty poets from certain
death.
And before that when I made a lake of wine
and turned tiny little fishes and dry loaves
into a Bacchanalian wedding feast. Remember

the dress you wore in the rain in Paris, how
the chill made your nipples burn with yearning.
Remember the smells of fresh buttered rolls
and coffee at that little bakery where we stopped
after making love. Remember it all—everything,
the totality of my soul and all it contained, all
the little sighs of submission, all the swallowed
screams of pleasure. Impossible, you say?

Impossible to remember everything, you say?
I've made it up, you say, turned myself into
my own myth. Well then, let me think…
Remember the time you wore that knit
dress, brushed past the back of my hand
and whispered, I love you. That happened,
didn't it? Or am I making it up? If so,
remember only that I loved you.

Dan Gilmore has published a novel, *A Howl for Mayflower* (Imago Press, 2006) and a collection of stories and poems, *Season Tickets* (Pima Press, 2003). He has received awards from the Raymond Carver Fiction Contest, the Martindale Fiction Award, and *Sandscript*. His poems have appeared in *Atlanta Review, Aethlon, Blue Collar Review, The Carolina Review, Rattle, Sandscript, OASIS Journal*, and *Still Crazy*. Several poems have been anthologized in *Loft and Range* (Pima Press, 2001).

Breinigsville, PA USA
19 April 2010
236454BV00001B/2/P